Miss Rhonda's Readers
Set THREE:

||||||||||||||||||||||||||||||||||||||||||||||||||||||||||||||||||||||||||||

Around Town
with Miss Rhonda

# Table of Contents

Goose on the Loose

In the spring, when a warm
wind blew, a "V" of geese
flew across the moon.
"Honk, honk, honk."

In the morning, a goose was
on the loose in the yard.

Miss Rhonda said, "Shoo, shoo!" to the goose and used the broom.

Sue the dog said,
"Woof, woof, woof!"
"Honk! Honk!" The goose
was very rude.

The goose rooted in the garden
and hid in the bushes.

In June, six new cute goslings
swam in the blue pool.

The goslings grew and grew,
and soon Miss Rhonda had
seven rude geese on the loose.

The geese flew in loops to the
river and back to the yard.

In the fall, when a cool wind blew, a "V" of geese flew across the moon.

In the morning, Miss Rhonda
had no goose on the loose.
Boo hoo!

Goose on the Loose
focus words:

ew	oo	u_e
· · · · ·	· · · · ·	· · · · · · ·
blew	moon	rude
flew	goose	used
new	loose	June
grew	woof	
	rooted	
	shoo	**ue**
	broom	· · · · ·
	pool	blue
	soon	Sue
	loops	
	cool	
	boo hoo	

The Brown
Mouse

On a cloudy spring day,
our cat sat by a mound
of dirt in our garden.

A little brown mouse was also
in the garden snacking on
sunflower seeds from a little
green pouch.

Our cat chased the mouse
across the garden and around
a watering can.

Just when the cat was about
to pounce, the little brown
mouse ran into our house.

The mouse ran around and around as Mom shouted louder and louder.

Our old hound howled and growled. He did not like the brown mouse in the house.

Our cat and dog chased the
mouse down the hall.

The mouse ran in back of
the couch and along the wall
without a sound.

Just when our cat was about
to pounce,

the little brown mouse ran out
of our house.

The Brown Mouse
focus words:

ow	**ou**	
shower	mouse	out
flower	cloudy	around
howled	ground	shouted
growled	about	louder
brown	house	hound
down	couch	our
	sound	without
	mound	pounce

Nosey
Goats

The goats want oats. They get
low and go slow. Oh no! The
goats get out of a hole.

The goats climb over a stone
wall. Oh no! They poke their
noses on the roses.

The goats roam in back of
Hope's window. They see a bar
of soap and yellow bowls in
the sink.

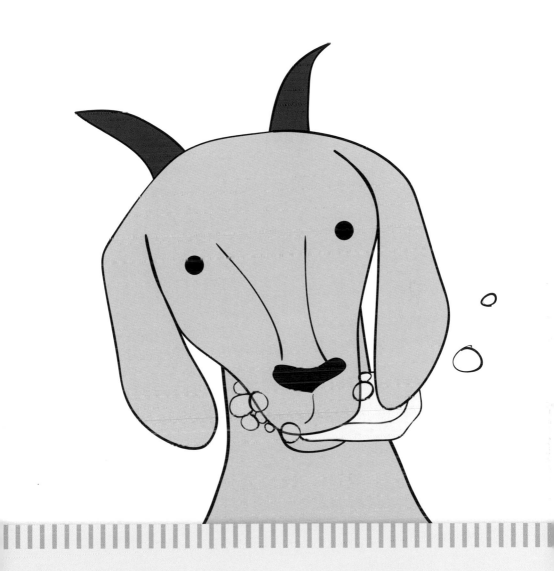

Oh no! A goat eats soap.

The goats go up a board.
They get in an old boat.

The boat tips over.
Oh no! The goats soar.

The goats run from Hope.
They run into a row of clothes.
Oh no! The goats wear coats.

The goats keep runnning.
They do not stop. Oh no!
The goats get in the road.

The goats go home in a row.
The goats are tied to a rope.

Oh no! The goats chew
their ropes.

Nosey Goats
focus words:

oa	**ow**	**o_e**
goat	low	poke
oats	slow	roses
roam	window	noses
soap	bowls	stone
board	yellow	Hope
boat	row	clothes
soar		home
coats		rope
road		

Clare and Daisy

Every Monday, Mom drives up
a shady lane to a big barn by
a lake.

Clare meets a pony named
Daisy. Daisy has a blaze in
the shape of a flower.

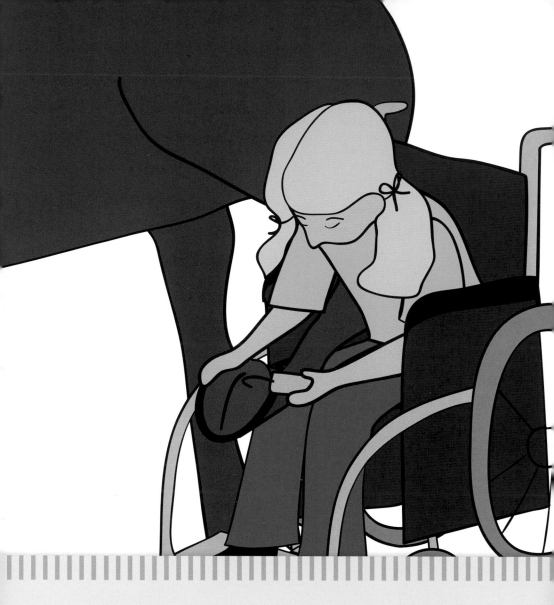

Clare learns how to take care
of Daisy. Clare checks Daisy's
hoof for rocks and dirt.

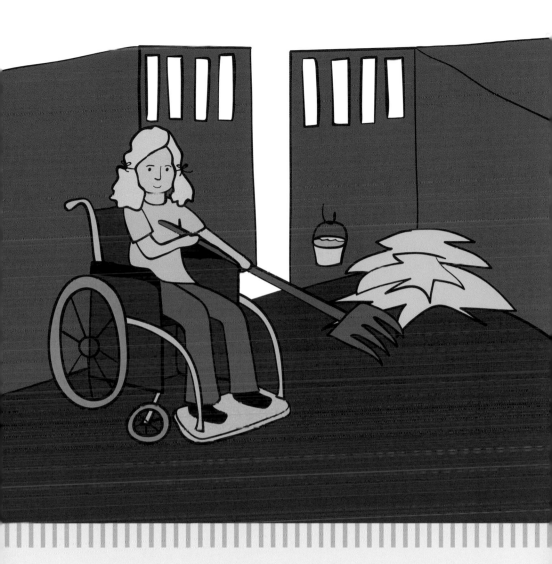

Clare rakes the stall and fills
a pail of water.

Clare feeds Daisy hay
and carrots.

Clare brushes Daisy and
braids her mane and tail
with red ribbons.

Clare wakes up on a sunny
Monday. She has been waiting
for this day!

Clare sees Daisy by the railing of the fence.

Clare gets in the saddle
and holds the reins.

Clare and Daisy take their
first ride on the trail.

Clare and Daisy
focus words:

ay	a_e	ai
Monday	Clare	Daisy
hay	lane	pail
day	lake	waiting
	blaze	railing
	shape	trail
a	care	
	rakes	
a	wakes	**ei**
shady		
		reins

Beavers

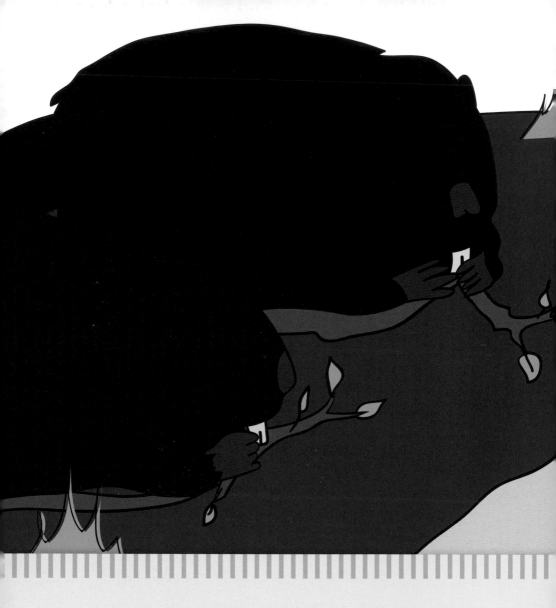

Two beavers meet along a
clear stream. They have a
meal of twigs, weeds and
leaves.

In the evening, they see an
empty valley. The beavers
begin to cut down trees with
their big teeth.

The beavers use the logs to
build a dam. They fill the
leaks with rocks, mud, sticks
and leaves.

When the pond is deep, they
begin to build a lodge.

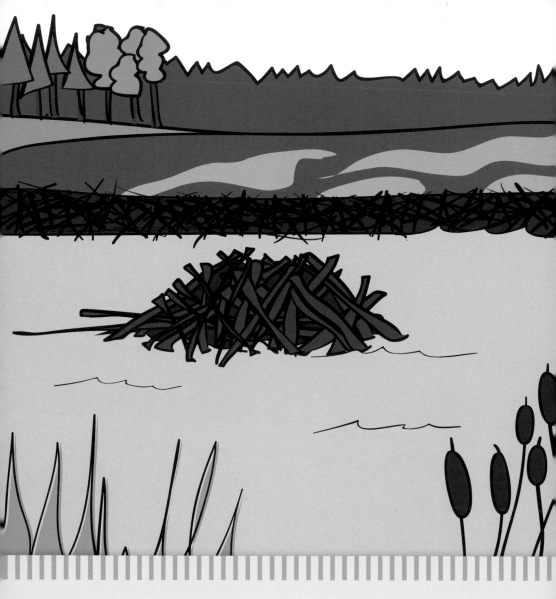

All summer, the busy beavers
work hard on their new home.

Many animals begin to visit
the new pond.

A beaver swims in the pond.
He sees a fox. Whap!
The beaver slaps his tail
on the water.

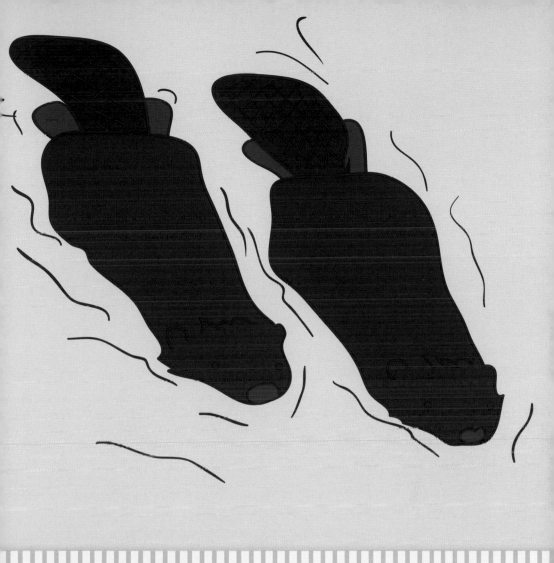

Both beavers swim fast
with their webbed feet.
They swim to their lodge.

In the winter, the beavers' thick fur keeps them warm. The mud and snow freeze the lodge solid and keep the beavers safe.

In the spring, the busy beavers
are ready for their new family.

Beavers
focus words:

ea	ee	y
.....	....	...
beaver	meet	empty
clear	weeds	valley
stream	see	busy
meal	trees	safety
leaves	teeth	ready
leaks	deep	many
	feet	family
	freeze	
	keeps	

e
...

begin

e_e
....

evening

Lights Out

At dinner time, pine needles
begin to fly by our window.

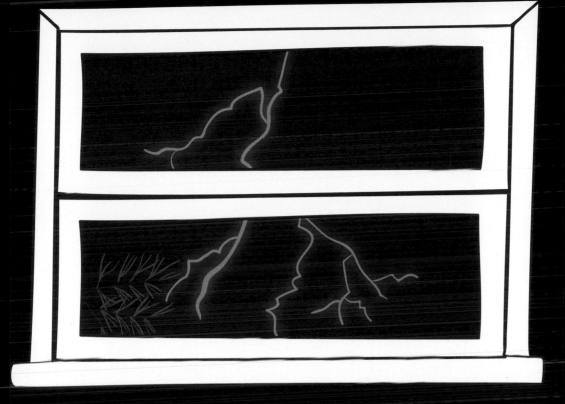

Flash! Crash! Lightning fills
the night sky, and the lights
go out in our house.

Mom says, "Sit tight. We will
be alright." She lights candles
and looks for a flashlight.

Dad's headlights shine in
the window as he turns
in the drive.

Mom lets us dine by the fire.

Dad makes a shadow of
a snail with his hands and
a flashlight.

We play hide and seek
with our flashlights.

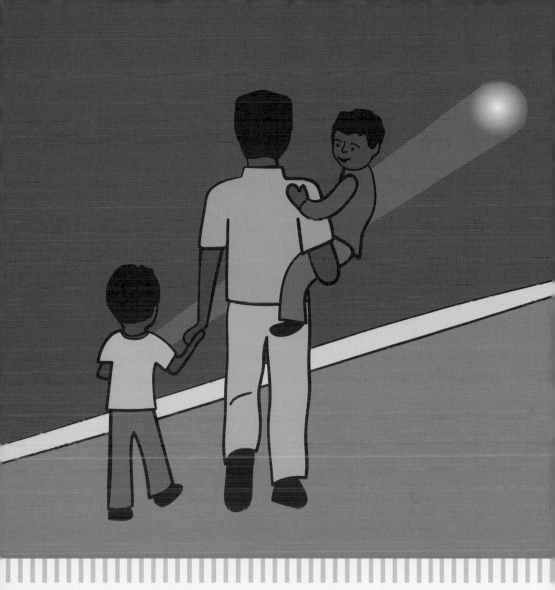

Dad gives Mike a ride to bed, and I shine the light.

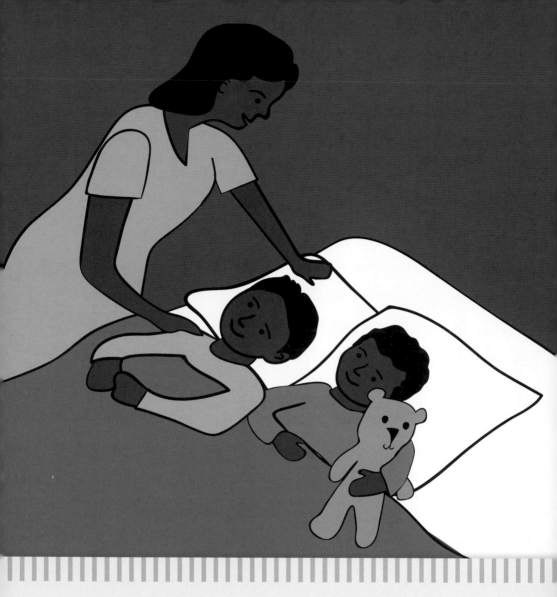

Mom tucks us in bed and
says, "Good night, sleep tight."

We lie snug in bed, side by
side. We smile. It has been
a good night.

Lights Out
focus words:

i_e	ie	igh
time	lie	lightning
pine		night
shine	**i**	lights
drive		tight
fire	I	alright
dine	behind	flashlight
hide		headlights
Mike		
ride		
side	**y**	
smile		
	fly	
	by	
	sky	

Caterpillar

In the fall, Miss Rhonda
gave a parsley plant to
her class. On the plant
was a little black caterpillar.

All week, the caterpillar got
bigger, and the parsley plant
got smaller.

On Saturday, when the
classroom was empty,
the caterpillar took a
walk across the room.

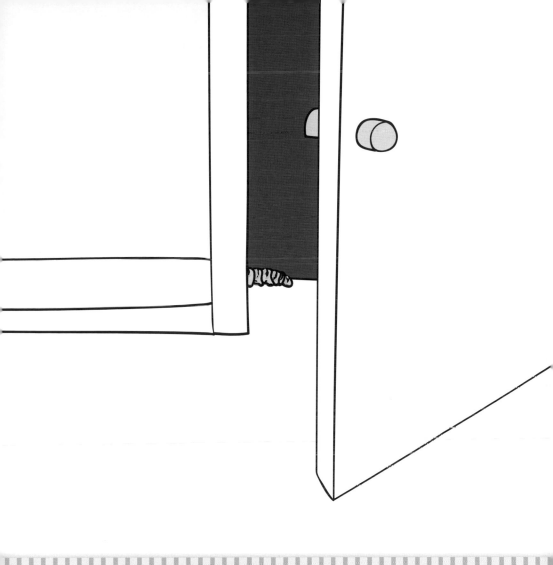

The caterpillar went into the
closet and did not come out.

On Monday, the children looked
for the missing caterpillar.

On Wednesday, there was a big rain storm. Miss Rhonda discovered a chrysalis in her red rain boots.

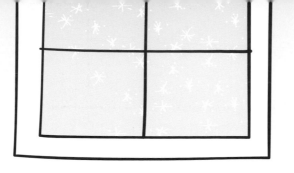

All winter, the chrysalis waited in the red boot. The children waited too.

In the spring, the children
planted parsley seeds in
small pots.

Sophia went to the closet for her gloves and watering can.

She came back with a black
swallowtail butterfly!

The children went outside to
see the butterfly fly away, and

then they planted the parsley
plants in the garden.

About the Creators

Rhonda Lucadamo is the real "Miss Rhonda" and the author of Miss Rhonda's Readers Sets ONE and TWO. She is an AMI Certified Montessori teacher and has taught young children for over 20 years.

Heidi Weathersby graduated from the Savannah College of Art and Design and works as a Graphic Designer. She lives in Atlanta with her husband, two daughters, a cat and two hamsters.

Jennifer Willhoite graduated from the University of Virginia and works as an illustrator and product designer. Jennifer lives with her husband, two daughters and their spaniel in Atlanta.